An Indiscreet Itinerary

You sail into a strange new world.

AN

Indiscreet Itinerary

OR

HOW THE UNCONVENTIONAL TRAVELER
SHOULD SEE HOLLAND

BY

ONE WHO WAS ACTUALLY BORN THERE
AND WHOSE NAME IS

Hendrik Willem van Loon

━━━

HARCOURT, BRACE AND COMPANY
NEW YORK

PRINTED IN THE UNITED STATES OF AMERICA
BY QUINN & BODEN COMPANY, INC., RAHWAY, N. J.
Typography by Robert S. Josephy

Janet darling,

You might as well read this little book. For even if you should never again leave your beloved Vermont, you will have to live with part of this ancient background for the rest of your days, and may they be many.

FATHER

Nieuw Amsterdam
4 April xxxiii

A
PERSONAL CONFESSION
TO THE READER

THIS little book is not at all what it set out
to be and I might just as well make a clean
breast of it and tell you the whole story.

The Netherlands Railways maintain an office
in New York at 405 Lexington Avenue and one
day their representative came to me and said:
"We have had endless folders about Holland and
some were good and some were not so good, but
anyway we thought we ought to have one written
by you. Whether you like it or not, you were a
Dutchman yourself once and you know the country inside out and outside in. Just to please us!
About six pages and a few of those funny little
pictures. You know what we mean!"

And in an unguarded moment I said "Yes"
(for I know pretty well what my beloved fellow-

countrymen think of my work), and I started to write this pamphlet, but then, to my great surprise, it started to write itself.

Now having spent most of my life traveling, I had long since realized that the time had come for a new sort of guide-book, but I had never paid much attention to the problem, having a sufficient number of other things to worry me, and here, without quite knowing what I was doing, I found myself writing exactly that new sort of guide-book about which I had been thinking for years.

When it was finished I went to my friends of the Netherlands Railways and I said: "Look here! You wanted a shrimp and I am giving you a whale. If you print this as a mere pamphlet, you know what will happen to it. Our dear public has had so many things given to it during the fat years of the last decade that now, whenever it suspects a 'given horse,' it no longer bothers to take it to the stable but deposits it straightway in the nearest ash-can. And be it said in all humility, this is really too good to be thrown away, so why don't you let me publish it as a regular guide-book, at so much per copy. If the est. public should like it sufficiently well to drop everything in hand and make straightway for the terrestrial Paradise I describe, so much the better for you, but if it proves a flop, then you merely say, 'Oh, well, just another one of those little van Loon books and you know what we think about them!' and no harm is done."

Well, after some very pleasant discussions and a little cabling and a few more cigarettes, all the difficulties were straightened out and "Pamphlet XY 4711 sub. B, series $9\frac{3}{4}$ to $11\frac{9}{17}$" became this "Indiscreet Itinerary" now published by Messrs. Harcourt, Brace and Co.

That is the way this little pamphlet, that became quite a book, had its origin, and here are the people in that country and this is the way they grew to be what they are and this is why they eat what they eat and drink what they drink and generally speaking, why they behave the way they behave—a short, personally conducted tour through unknown territory, together with a few handy hints for those who want to see strange lands, whether at home and in their own armchair, or from the windows of the Netherlands

Railways, of whom I remain, with gratitude for their suggestion, the very humble and obedient servant,

HENDRIK WILLEM VAN LOON

Nieuw Amsterdam,
4 March xxxiii.

An Indiscreet Itinerary

THE BACKGROUND
AGAINST WHICH TO SEE
THE FOREGROUND

A LL ROADS," so the Middle Ages said, "lead to
Rome."

We no longer live in the seventeenth century
when for a short six decades all roads traveled by
artists, writers, scientists, statesmen and soldiers
led to Holland. But even today those who visit
northern Europe cannot very well avoid catch-
ing at least a short glimpse of the Kingdom of
the Netherlands, which continues to be the center (and in some ways, the heart) of the civilization that early during the thirteenth century
sprang up around the North Sea and that since
then has put its stamp upon every part of the
world.

Now I do not intend to make this an historical
treatise, but there is no use visiting a country

3

unless you know the how and why and wherefore of its existence. And so, first of all, a few words in which to explain why a former strip of mud-flats and marshlands could develop into a nation which played a rôle in the cultural and political development of our globe so absurdly out of proportion to its actual size that one has to go back to the days of Athens to find its exact counterpart.

The North Sea, which you will have to cross in order to get from America or England to the northern part of the European continent, is one of the youngest of all larger bodies of water. Long after the first plants and trees and animals from the heart of Europe had crossed dry-shod to England, that sea was formed. In those days, the Thames flowed into the Rhine and the Rhine flowed through eastern England, as you may see to this very day by following its ancient river bed on a geological map.

After the great natural catastrophe which caused the formation of the British Channel, the North Sea became a vast expanse of water which connected the Arctic Ocean with the Gulf of Biscay. But its very shallowness betrays its origin as so much "inundated land." If you happen to be on deck a few hours before you stop to take on the pilot, you will be surprised at the vast number of light-ships and buoys which you pass and at the occasional sudden zigzagging of your vessel. You are really sailing through narrow gulleys between endless invisible sand-banks. Yachting on the North Sea is a grand sport but a very difficult and dangerous one.

The final submerging process of all this dry land was probably due to a long series of exceptionally wet summers. The rivers that came from the east must have carried millions of tons of extra water and mud down to the sea in their search for an outlet. When normal climatic conditions returned, all that remained above the surface of the waves was a long, narrow strip of sand-dunes and behind this strip an endless waste of marshes which reached all the way down from those dunes to the great Central European Plain, the final outskirts of which you will meet as soon as you get east of Utrecht or when you follow the railroad between Dordrecht and Roosendaal.

This marshland was an ideal territory for strag-

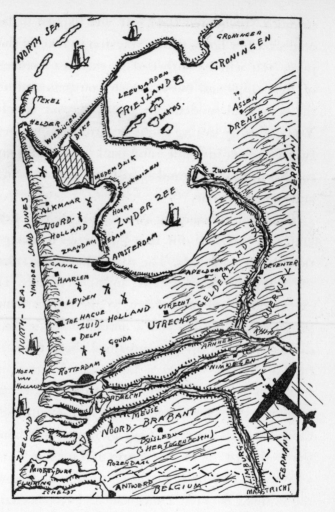

The big rivers here leave the northern European plain
and form the low delta which became Holland.

glers from the mainland, a sort of vast lagoon closely resembling the territory occupied by those fugitives from the Adriatic shores who founded Venice. About a hundred years before the birth of Christ, certain Germanic tribes came floating down the Rhine. (The Rhine is a queer river. It has 12,000 tributaries, a record which few other streams can beat.) Those early immigrants established themselves on the few bits of dry territory that were situated between the branches of the Meuse and the Rhine proper and which of course were very fertile. Others, attracted by the rumor of "free land," appeared upon the scene. The stronger ones survived. The weaker brethren moved westward. Life was beginning to be "normal" and then one day the first of the Roman explorers appeared upon the scene.

The Rhine and the Meuse and the Scheldt were found to be convenient routes to England for the purpose of transporting troops and merchandise. The Romans knew very little geography in the modern sense of the word. They were not in the least scientific in the way they drew their maps. Nevertheless when it came to finding a short and

Even on a fairly quiet day you will be surprised to see
what a turbulent spot "Holland's Furthest West" is.

direct route between two points, they were just as intelligent as the most up-to-date of modern engineers. If perchance you should visit the village of Domburg in the southern part of Holland on the island of Walcheren, you will notice that it is the spot where the cable to England plunges into the North Sea. On that very same spot, as we have since discovered, the bottom of the sea is thickly covered with fragments of old Roman statuary. Those bits of stone and clay are the remnants of little votive statues which the Romans offered to their Gods once they had safely crossed that turbulent ocean, which never ceased to inspire these landlubbers from the Mediterranean with a most dreadful fear. You see how this bears out my point. Domburg was the exact spot from which the Roman legions sailed for England. Somehow or other their engineers had discovered that this part of the Low Countries was the most convenient jumping-off-place for those who intended to try their luck among the painted but docile savages of Britain.

As for the original settlers of the low marshlands of Holland, according to the very meagre

In the popular imagination of that day that obstinate
courage expressed itself in the figure of The Flying
Dutchman.

chronicles of that time, they offered but a weak resistance to the Romans and after a few futile outbreaks of discontent, they willingly enough accepted the Roman system which meant taxes and jails but also roads and canals and dykes and security. After four centuries, however, the Barbarians from eastern Europe began to overrun Rome in all seriousness. The outlying military posts were hastily called home to defend the Mother City. And the Low Countries were left to the mercy of the Viking, a person who looks eminently picturesque in fiction but who was nothing but an organized gangster with eagle feathers on his head instead of a gray Fedora hat.

Then during the eighth and ninth centuries of our era, the first Christian missionaries appeared upon the scene and soon cloisters were being built all over the place, and that meant a return of civilization and a rebuilding of those roads and canals and dykes which ever since the departure of the Romans had fallen into complete and disastrous neglect, a neglect which had led up to the disasters which caused the formation of the

In contrast to the low western part, the eastern part of
the country consists of rolling moorland.

Zuyder Zee and many of the wide estuaries in the south.

But in spite of some very mild return of prosperity, the Low Countries, during the whole of the earlier part of the Middle Ages, were but a negligible quantity in the eyes of the rest of the world, a foggy and inhospitable land of fishermen and peasants, administered by a few local and rather crude feudal gentlemen who were desperately trying to put some order into the chaos left behind by the centuries of anarchy that had followed in the wake of Rome's downfall.

All of this, of course, held true only of the northern part of the Low Countries. The southern part, or Belgium, which had become much more thoroughly Romanized than the cold and damp northern regions, had become a veritable center of provincial civilization, but the north was just plain "back woods," a hinterland which was suspected of being the last stopping place before you reached the end of the world and established connections with the walruses and the Eskimos.

And then quite suddenly and unexpectedly a miracle happened. An economic miracle, to be ex-

In the interior the landscape has changed remarkably
little since the sixteenth century.

act. The herring, bless his little cold heart! decided to move from the Baltic into the North Sea. Next a bright young Zeeland fisherman devised a method of curing and packing the useful *Clupea harengus* in such a way that it could be used for purposes of export. Then the North Sea proved to be a gold mine, if I may mix my metaphors just a little.

The Middle Ages, with their very limited menu and their endless holidays and fast-days when no meat was allowed to be eaten, most heartily welcomed this new dish on the monotonous bill of fare of bread and meat and no vegetables (they did not make their appearance until long after the Crusades). Suddenly the low marshes along the banks of the North Sea found themselves possessed of a most profitable monopoly, almost as valuable as the salt monopoly which had given Venice its original start in the world and which had allowed that proud Republic to defy both emperor and pope.

The money accumulated from the herring fisheries was quietly invested in larger and more seaworthy vessels and during the seasons when the herring was busy raising its family and had descended to the deepest parts of the ocean where the primitive nets of that day could not follow it, the ships of Holland and Zeeland and Friesland and all the other little principalities traveled to the Baltic to get loaded to the gunwales with the grain from Poland and from Russia which they then carried to France and Spain and to the countries of the Mediterranean where an exhausted soil would no longer produce enough to support the ever increasing population.

It has been said and truly so that Amsterdam was built on herring-bones. And the same holds true of a large number of other Dutch cities. The first signs of prosperity they ever enjoyed were fished out of the grayish-green North Sea. Then came the grain trade, which dealt with the necessities of life and therefore allowed the Dutch to make all sorts of profits. Meanwhile another change was sweeping over the country. A seafaring life and combined with that a sense of independence which was born out of living in a large number of very small cities, each one, however, strong enough to defy the local counts and dukes and barons with almost sublime impudence, had caused the development of a spirit of physical and spiritual liberty which was entirely out of place in an age which watched the consolidation of all the great dynastic holdings of western and northern Europe into a few large kingdoms and empires.

If you want to study this subject a little more seriously, take a copy of Motley's "Rise of the Dutch Republic" with you on your trip across the ocean. I know it is rather an old-fashioned book but it still makes excellent reading. You can skip certain parts of the political preliminaries which will probably rather bore you but when you come to the struggle for freedom itself, then you will find Motley as interesting as the best of our modern adventure stories.

Perhaps I had better make it part of the prescribed reading of the voyage for I cannot here enter into the details of that ever memorable struggle between the Low Countries and their absentee landlord, King Philip of Habsburg and of Spain and of almost all the out-lying real estate of the entire globe. The war lasted eighty years or three entire generations. The first twenty years were terrible. But almost fifteen centuries of fighting the forces of Nature had given these fishermen and traders and skippers and farmers a strain of obstinacy which made them say, "No! We will rather cut dykes and let the whole land drown than give in to that foreign potentate with the big jaw who lives a thousand miles away from us yet undertakes to tell us what we should think and do and, most of all, what we should believe." And eventually this obstinacy was to become their greatest strength as often, alas, it has degenerated into their greatest weakness. Obstinacy (I know it, for I have my share) is not entirely a pleasant quality but like all the less amiable qualities of the mind and the soul, it is a mighty useful one when you are trying to survive in a world full of a number of things, but most of them not so good.

In the year 1648 the Republic finally gained its independence. But during the previous eighty years, the pressure from the outside had been so terrific and the resistance necessary to withstand that pressure had been so tremendous that in this instance peace caused a veritable explosion of pent-up energy and enthusiasm and courage and piety and faith and endurance and a rough but wholesome joy-of-life which made the contemporaries of Rembrandt and Prince Maurice feel, "The world is our oyster. Let us have a couple of dozen and let us have them right away."

It is really a little ludicrous to sit before a map of our planet and then follow the progress of the Dutch across the Seven Seas. You will find a Staten Island off New York and one off the Strait of Magellan, which as you know runs parallel with the wide open spaces south of Cape Horn, also a short cut to the Dutch Indies and called by the discoverer after the little city of Hoorn on the Zuyder Zee. You will find the remnants of a small wooden Dutch house on the northernmost tip of Nova Zembla (hopping-off place for the North Pole) as a reminder that the Dutch seriously contemplated finding a route of their own to the Indies by way of northern Asia. And you will see funny-looking little houses with steep roofs (as a precaution against a heavy snowfall) when you enter the harbor of Curaçao in the West

Indies. You still may dig up the tin plates which Abel Tasman left on the coast of Australia when he first explored that continent and the New Zealand of Maori fame is called after the old Zeeland where I have spent so many happy years of my life.

If you study the history of the island of Deshima, just off the city of Nagasaki, you will be surprised to learn that for 217 years, during which Japan was supposed to be closed to all foreign influences, the Dutch succeeded in keeping the door just sufficiently ajar to let at least a tiny bit of western light trickle into the far-off realm of the Shogun. You will find a President of the United States living in a village on the Hudson which still bears its original name of Kromme Elboog, or Curved Elbow, and you will hear the best families of Brazil boast about their Dutch origin. You will come across the remnants of a Dutch whaling town on Spitzbergen and you will find Dutch graveyards on Jan Mayen Island, just east of Greenland, and on Formosa, just east of China, and on Ceylon, just south of British India, all of them former Dutch colonies. You may follow the traces of a special Dutch postal service that crossed India and Persia and Asia Minor and that followed about the same route now taken by the mail and passenger planes of the Royal Dutch Airmail on its weekly trips from Amsterdam to Batavia (eight days, compared to the year and a half which it took the first Dutch vessels to reach Java).

The island of Mauritius between Madagascar and India will remind you of that Prince Maurice of Nassau (son of William the Silent) who bestowed his name upon rivers and islands all over the map and after whom, originally, the Hudson River was called.

But you would make a serious mistake if you thought that you were about to visit merely another one of those Museums of Historical Curiosities of which Europe is so full today. A great deal of territory has been lost, as was quite natural when a country of a million and a half tried to lord it over the entire globe. But a great deal also has been retained and after a few days in The Hague and in Amsterdam you will begin to feel in some subtle, mysterious way that you are still in the heart of a vast colonial empire. The Cape is no longer part of the old Dutch possessions, although it had retained (and is rapidly regaining) its old Dutch tongue and character. In the New World only half a dozen islands and a bit of land in South America tell of the days when Nieuw Amsterdam and Fort Orange (now called Albany) were trading posts of the Dutch West India Company. But a territory so vast that it would cover the map of Europe from Gibraltar to the Ural Mountains in Eastern Russia, or from Seattle to the shores of Georgia, is still in Dutch hands.

How they have managed to hold on quite so long and quite so successfully, I do not know. Sheer force does not account for it, for the moment these colonies, outnumbering the mother-country almost ten to one, made up their mind to push the "foreigner" into the sea, they could do so. I have never been there but I am willing to accept the judgment of some very shrewd observers. "A mixture of obstinacy tempered by common sense has done it," they tell me and I am inclined to believe that they are right. For "obstinacy tempered by common sense" has been the political and spiritual slogan of these people ever since they established themselves as an independent nation. It was obstinacy which made them—it was common sense which showed them the value of turning their country into a haven of refuge for all the oppressed of the world.

This policy of the open door to all those who found life intolerable in their own home made Holland the melting-pot of the seventeenth and eighteenth centuries. French Huguenots and Portuguese Jews and German dissenters from the Habsburg domains and Englishmen and Scotchmen who for political and religious reasons were forced to leave their own towns and villages brought to their new fatherland their courage and their energy and their ability and greatly helped in making the young Republic the center of the arts and of science and of commerce.

That the Puritans who eventually were to drift to the shores of Massachusetts found this country highly uncongenial is a well-known historical fact. But it is doubtful whether they would have fitted in anywhere else with more chance of success. Their Dutch hosts were willing enough to let them live in peace, provided however they ceased to be hyphenated citizens (and proud of it, too) and not try to get exempted from military service. As these excellent Children of Zion had no intention of changing from what they were (fanatical little middle-class English farmers and shop-keepers) they could only expect to find perfection when they were alone and so they moved on to the New World.

Please do not conclude from what I have just said that Holland was a sort of terrestrial Heaven, populated exclusively by pure and unselfish little angels and saints. The Dutch of the seventeenth century were no better and no worse than their neighbors. In many respects they were probably worse but they had gone through a terrible personal experience which had given them a first-hand knowledge of those miseries which follow in the wake of religious strife and in the second place, they were merchants, first, last and all the time, and they realized that a man who wants to do business with all the world cannot afford to

24

ask every one of his customers what he thinks and why and wherefore.

In regard to their own dissenters (and the Dutch have always been great at dissenting) those unfortunate heretics were rigorously excluded from participation in all affairs of state. But provided that they observed what a very wise mayor of New York once called "an outer form of order and decency," they were not molested as you may see for yourself (if you are interested in that sort of thing) by visiting those curious "attick churches" of Amsterdam where even the Catholics could foregather in a state of semi-public secrecy and read mass, a procedure quite unimaginable in any other purely Protestant country.

By far the greater part of the immigrants were among the staunchest friends of the new commonwealth and out of this unexpected mixture of races and creeds, a new nation was born which in the realm of medicine and mathematics and philosophy and pharmacy and practically all the arts and sciences easily established itself within a remarkably short space of time as the leading country of the day.

But here again I am not merely talking of the past. The fact that a few years ago in the University of Leyden one could call on four recipients of the Nobel prize within five minutes' walk (if they would open their doors to you, but most of the time they were too busy), shows that the old spirit of scientific enthusiasm has not yet died. Those visitors, especially interested in the social development of a modern state, in housing problems and insurance for the aged and the sick will soon notice that they have not entered a museum of historical curiosities but that they are living in a community which on a small scale does all those things which large countries are only too apt to neglect on a much larger scale.

So much for the general historical background against which you must see this country if you want to judge it according to its merits and not merely according to its appeal of the picturesque. You may not always be able to recognize these excellent achievements at first sight, for the Dutch, like most northern races, are not much given to advertising their own wares. On the contrary, they will usually try to deprecate their own virtues as much as possible. In their daily lives they are probably the most conservative nation of Europe. That, as I have said before, is their greatest weakness as well as their greatest strength.

But if you want to profit from your travels, you might just as well learn at the very beginning that it does not pay to look in the different countries for what is not there. When you are in Holland, do not expect to find the pleasant qualities of Italy and vice versa. The inhabitants of a country where it rains three days out of every seven are not much given to singing merry tunes in the market place. No, they are apt to be an indoor people. I do not mean in regard to sports, for sport, during the last thirty years, has made tremendous headway among all the classes of society. But Holland is one of the few countries where the "home" in the old sense of the word has survived until today. And that home is usually a self-sufficient unit. It may open its doors to you but not until long acquaintance has convinced those on the inside that those on the outside will actually fit into the particular little cosmos that is hidden behind those empty windows of the front room, which seem so dead and lifeless that you wonder whether the house is really inhabited.

A train in Holland does not become the happy house-party of a train in our own West. It is merely a convenient method of rapid transportation, consisting of small compartments wherein everybody peruses his own particular hobbies and newspaper. But even those newspapers closely reflect the particular point of view of their readers in regard to their religious, social and political, artistic and scientific convictions. For among those tremendous individualists everybody, high and low, is entitled to his own views. As a result, even conversation becomes a sort of spiritual and intellectual "each man for himself." It is a bit dull but it has one great advantage. It gives each person a better chance to develop his own particular characteristics.

The standard of learning and general information is high. In matters of music and science it is so high that the professional musicians and scientists find this a veritable haven of appreciation. The tourist, not bound upon such a high mission, will sometimes feel that he is somewhat out of the picture. But when he keeps it before his eyes that this country was born out of an everlasting struggle between Nature and Man, and that that struggle never for a single moment can be relaxed, then he will begin to appreciate that these people are only what their historical and geographical environment has made them, just as we ourselves and everybody else that draws breath.

The Dutch system of survival has its disadvantages, but by and large, it has also definite advantages. It has allowed a comparatively small nation to survive and to do much more than its actual share of the world's work because it has been able to keep itself intact from foreign influences. All this may not make for a great deal of charm nor for a very colorful existence nor for the cheerful laughter and the easy-come and easy-go of southern climes. But it brings about a certain steadiness of purpose of the whole of the community. There was really a grain of truth in that old devise of the House of Orange, "We will maintain." Revaluated into the terms of every-

This country is never dull. For where there is water,
there also is life.

day life, that slogan, during the last five centuries, seems to have come to mean "We will maintain ourselves as best pleases us." And behold! the system works.

A great deal of water has washed through the mouth of the Rhine and the Meuse since William of Orange placed himself at the head of the rebellion that eventually was to lead up to national independence. The country, since then, has had its ups and downs. But very little seems ever to have really affected these placid burghers who are never in a hurry, who in the year of speed 1933 walk as unconcernedly through the traffic of a modern city as if they were still smoking a peaceful pipe on some village street, who ponderously work their way through immense newssheets telling them everything about the great big world and yet never feel themselves to be an integral part of that great big world, who through a haze of astonished "Well-you-don't-say-so's," listen to all the "goings-on" of a universe that has gone positively crazy and who, at the same time, maintain the best equipped air-lines, who pay their debts (both at home and abroad), who in a

Please remember that it is not strictly necessary to eat everything you will find on the Dutch breakfast table. It is not the only meal of the day!

bankrupt world enjoy all the credit they need, who build and navigate ships that amble along like canal-boats yet always get there, and who, after a lifetime spent in ruling foreign lands as large as Great Britain or Italy, can return contentedly to their own placid canals and spend the rest of their days tending the cabbages and the tulips in their own back yards.

I am not saying that this is the Good Life or that we in America could or should try to change our own standards to those of the Low Countries. But in the perplexing world of today where no values remain the same from one week till the next, where governments change with the rapidity of headlines in a tabloid and where a thousand novel ideas and ideals and theories are forever being tried and are forever being found wanting, it is rather refreshing to visit one tiny corner of the planet where a Queen can still leave her palace to go forth and attend to her own errands without being accompanied by a phalanx of secret service men; where bank-runners can drop into a saloon for a peaceful glass of beer without bothering about the cash they carry under their arms;

33

where a Bolshevist agitator can make a public speech and denounce the Royal Family and the entire existing order of things in the most preposterous terms and get no further reaction beyond an indifferent shrug of the shoulders and the casual remark, "Aw, shucks! the fellow is crazy"; where that good five-cent cigar of Vice President Marshall is still to be had for the equivalent of five cents; where people eat for the fun of it and not for the calories; where dominies are able to fulminate against a hapless Zeppelin that flies across their country on a Sunday as a messenger from the Devil (because it makes people forget the Sabbath Day and its quiet holiness); where birth control advocates are not thrown into the hoosegow; where careful farmers grow radishes on the sides of railroad dykes, while their sons or cousins are able to throw the fear of God into our own oil-magnates by the threat of a rate-war; where the price of rubber and tobacco is dictated by people who go to the office with a ham sandwich in their pockets; where the army is considered a joke and where part of that army is forever engaged in war;

where a postoffice employee can sell you a stamp with more deliberation than a glacier during a very cold winter and will then connect you with some distant station in Java in less than five minutes and at one third of the cost of a three-minute talk to New York (which is so much nearer); where everything is new and yet old and where nobody ever seems to get excited about any problem except that eminently practical question that faces all of us, "Does it work?"

HOW TO GET THERE
AND WHAT TO DO
ONCE YOU ARRIVE

T HE FIRST thing to do once you arrive in any
place is to sit down and catch your breath
and take a nap if you feel so inclined. All boat
schedules conspire against a peaceful night's sleep
on the part of the traveler. I suppose this is un-
avoidable. The Harwich line must catch the early
morning connection with Germany and central
Europe. The boats of the Holland-America Line
(if you happen to go directly from New York to
Rotterdam) must still pay some attention to the
tides and currents which (as we all know) respect
the comfort of no one, and the Batavier Line,
which connects London directly with Rotterdam
(the oldest regular steamboat line in Europe, I
believe) finds it to its advantage to dock some
time before the beginning of the business day.

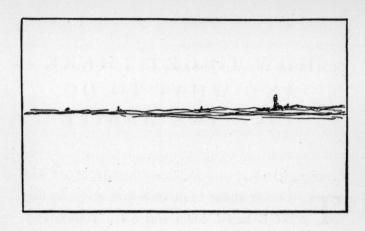

What you see first of all.

And of course, if you are at all of a curious nature, you will have been up long before the boat comes within sight of the shore. And you will be fully repaid for your troubles.

First of all you will see a thin, dark line which is a different sort of darkness from both sky and sea and which at irregular intervals is pierced with blinding streaks of light which flash across the water like seagulls diving for a fish. That is that row of sand-dunes which since three thousand years ago has protected the country against the inroads of the North Sea. Then the vessel will do some plain and fancy zigzagging for it must make directly for the narrow gap between two distant breakwaters, and the currents between the sand-banks are infinitely more treacherous than those of our own Hudson River, while the tides are almost equally bad.

Meanwhile your eyes will have become accustomed to the darkness and then suddenly the thought will strike you: "But this is absurd! We are sailing right above the roofs of the houses." But it is not absurd. You have quietly slipped inside the breakwater. You are now on the river

The dunes, the lonely guardians of the land.

and all the land on both sides of you is from ten to fifteen feet below the surface of the sea.

As the day dawns above the horizon, you will notice other unfamiliar scenes. On both sides of you are pastures and contemplative cows look solemnly at the black shadow that drifts past them and then return to the infinitely more important task of getting their breakfast. It may be your business to leave a comfortable home and go a-cruising all over the world. Just then, it is their business to eat. So there!

And the occasional kids that walk along the dykes seem to belong to the same school of placid philosophy. When you enter New York harbor on a summery day, every cat-boat filled with pleasure seekers starts into wild jubilations as if you were a long-lost son and your ship the long-awaited Ark of Righteousness. The Dutch infants, bound so early in the morning for the bakery or for school, are differently constructed. They do not want to be unfriendly. By no means. When you wave at them, they will wave back. But you probably have some perfectly good reason to be on that vessel at that particular moment, just as

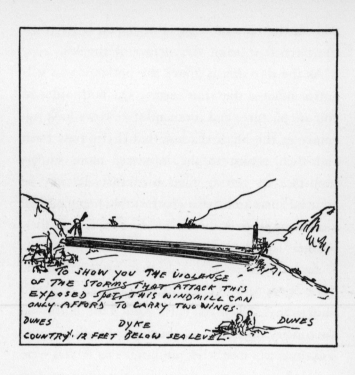

At Westkapelle you can see, better than anywhere else, what a dyke really means to these low countries.

they have a perfectly good reason to be on their little dyke at that particular moment. So why make a fuss about it?

Meanwhile the vessel has slowed down from half-speed to a fraction of no-speed-at-all. When you look behind you, you will at once notice the reason. The company does not want to be held responsible for the inundation of the entire country and the harmonious waves driven up by your 25,000 tons are licking the tops of the dykes.

But then at last there is something familiar—factories! Industrialism is rarely pretty. But the stone barracks and the ship wharves and the high smoke-stacks have not been quite able to destroy the old picturesque views of this river which probably for the first time in your life makes you realize the painstaking truth of those Dutch landscapes of the seventeenth century which you have already seen in our own museums.

Now, if you will look far forward, you will notice the outline of an old tower surrounded by a cluster of houses and trees. That is the town of Brielle where the great rebellion started in 1572 (read your Motley). It is now a country village

43

The first sign of human habitation which you see is the
gigantic tower of the old city of Brielle.

but it happens to be one of those spots of which one can say, with a slight variation, Pascal's famous dictum about the nose of Cleopatra ("If the nose of Cleopatra had been one tenth of an inch different, the whole subsequent history of the world would have been different too"): "If it had not been for the presence of that little city at the mouth of the Rhine, the entire history of the last four hundred years would have been changed."

And then, on the left, you will see what used to be the village of Delfshaven, famous as the spot where the Pilgrims set forth to go to England where they were to be reloaded into the leaky holds of the "Speedwell" and the "Mayflower," bound for the vague but profitable tobacco fields of Virginia. The "Speedwell" did not speed quite as well, as you may remember, and had to return. The "Mayflower," less lucky, exposed its unhappy cargo to endless weeks of seasickness and then landed them in New England, too miserable to bother about any further pioneering.

After Delfshaven, the traffic grows heavier and a vast number and variety of small cargo boats

All the water that comes down has to come out again.

begin to play hide-and-seek with their big trans-
atlantic sisters, for Holland is still a country
where the bulk of all hauling is done by means of
canal-boats. A few years ago Henry Ford visited
the Netherlands and in an outburst of progress
suggested in all seriousness that the canals be
filled with sand and be turned into motor high-
roads. That these waterways are at the same time
drainage canals and that the country would drown
the moment they ceased to exist had escaped the
eminent interior-combustion expert.

But since we are on the subject and very few
people seem to know how the so-called "polders"
of Holland are made, I might as well tell you in
just as few words as possible.

Most of the reclaiming was done in the sixteenth century, after the "water-mill," the wind-
driven pumping-station, had been sufficiently per-
fected to be of some practical use. Well, when
you want to get rid of a lake, you first of all build
a stout dyke around the whole of the marsh or
lake you intend to tackle. Then you dig a canal
outside that dyke and erect a dozen pumping-
stations along it. They will suck the water out of

OF COURSE THEY NEVER BOTHERED ABOUT LITTLE BITS OF WATER LIKE THIS BUT JUST TO GIVE YOU AN IDEA HOW IT IS DONE —

Polder No. 1.

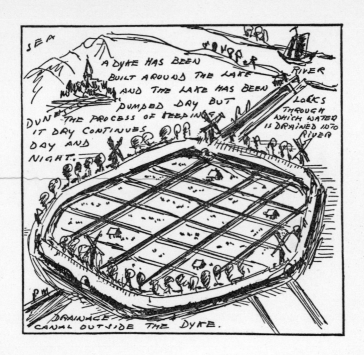

Polder No. 11.

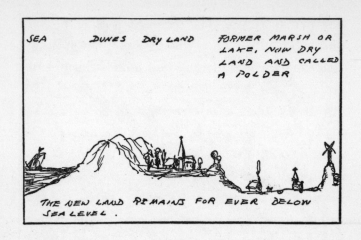

SEA   DUNES   DRY LAND   FORMER MARSH OR LAKE, NOW DRY LAND AND CALLED A POLDER

THE NEW LAND REMAINS FOR EVER BELOW SEA LEVEL.

Polder No. III.

the marsh as you suck lemonade out of a glass through a straw. Then you dig a number of drainage canals inside the dried-up land, in neat little squares, and the pumping-stations (now mostly driven by steam or electricity) will do the rest.

And what becomes of the water pumped out of your erstwhile lake? That in turn is poured into still other canals which finally by means of locks connect with one of the big rivers. When the tide is low and the water in your canals is high, you open the locks and get rid of the superfluous water. If you need water in your canals, as you may during very hot summers, you reverse the process. It is really very simple if you know how.

After another hour houses begin to multiply. So do bicycles. As soon as daylight appears, the Dutch bicycles appear. If there really is anything in all this talk about evolution, another century will see the Dutch children coming into this world on tiny bicycles. There are automobiles too in Holland, but the bicycle has become an integral part of the native technological fauna. Ambitious youngsters will begin to race your ship on their bicycles as soon as they spy you from afar.

Butcher-boys, delivering their errands, will do the same. Baker-boys will do the same. Policemen will do the same. The harbor pilot is the only citizen who comes to you decently and ceremoniously in a little boat of his own. And now, all around you, there are ships and more ships, varying from a few cubic feet to twenty or thirty thousand tons. But they all behave in an essentially Dutch way. They mind their own business. So as a rule do the customs people who are the first of the natives to welcome you.

Now that the whole world has become one large community, every nation has flattered us by erecting some sort of customs barrier of its own around all its frontiers. Holland, the traditional country of free trade, has been forced to become a tariff country. But the customs people still feel slightly apologetic about inquiring into the sort of luggage you have chosen to bring with you. It is a detail, but a detail which shows that in one respect at least they are a great deal wiser than most of our eminent statesmen and politicians.

Landing on foreign soil (or domestic soil for that matter, only more so) means standing around

and getting tired and irritated and wondering what the funny new currency is like. Dutch currency however is very easy. The standard coin is a ryksdaalder, which looks and behaves like our own dollar. But bills are presented in guilders or florins (so-called after a certain Count Floris of Holland, who first coined them in the thirteenth century). A guilder is approximately forty cents in our money (unless we decide to "inflate," in which case it will be a lot more). The easiest way to keep track of your expenses is by multiplying the Dutch cost-price by 4 and then moving the decimal point one point towards the left. For example, when something costs you 5.20 guilders, you multiply that 5.20 by 4 which makes it f 20.80. (The sign for a guilder or florin is an f.) Move the decimal point one point towards the left and you get $2.08 in American currency (f 3.75 = $1.50, f 1.90 = $.76).

On the whole, while the country is not cheap, you need not fear that they will add the current date of the month to your bill. And there is no use trying to bargain in the average Dutch store any more than you would do at Macy's or Marshall Field's.

As for tipping, ten percent and a shade over, if you are well satisfied, will settle that problem once and for all. By the way, don't try to tip the customs people. It does not always work at home and it does not work in western Europe at all. Don't try to tip cops. A street-car conductor who tells you how to get somewhere or who changes a bill of large denomination for you may accept a tip or a cigar. But other officials are "state employees." That may not mean much to you but it means a lot to them.

And another "by the way." If you have brought your own car, you might just as well avail yourself when trying to cross a city of one of those insistent urchins who devote themselves to that particular racket. Those Dutch cities are as complicated as downtown Boston and you will save yourself a lot of trouble by hiring one of the ragamuffins to guide you. Pay him half of what he asks and he will still grin at you as an easy mark. But you are traveling, so who cares? And once outside the cities, the Dutch bicycle club will take you in hand and it will watch over your every step as no mother, however careful, has ever guided the destiny of her best-beloved child. Holland is about the best "sign-posted" country in Europe and you will remember this regretfully as soon as you have gone to France or Belgium. On literally every corner of every road you will find a sign-post with the correct distance to the next village. The distances are in kilometers. Inches and yards and the other hopeless complexities of the muddle-headed Middle Ages are definitely left behind, once you reach the continent. I can't tell you how to revaluate kilometers into miles. Ask Einstein. He may know, but I doubt it. (He does. A kilometer is ⅝ of a mile. 80 KM is 50 miles. Hence, multiply the number of KM by 6 and shade it up a trifle. 17 KM would be between 10 and 10½ miles. A.E.)

And now cometh the question, Whither are we bound? I suppose that you are traveling by yourself and not in a group. In the latter case, you save yourself all the worry of a trip and you also miss most of the fun. A trip to a foreign country should be a voyage of discovery. That means the

Finally above the masts and the smokestacks there looms a tower. It is the tower of the St. Lawrence Church of Rotterdam.

occasional missing of trains, though even that is unlikely if you are willing to look at a few time-tables and the time-tables are just the same as ours except that the mis-leading A.M. and P.M. have been dropped and that the clock in Europe now runs on a 24 hour schedule. (Deduct 12 and you get the P.M. time. 17:35 means 17:35— 12 in our time, or 5:35 P.M.)

Well, the chances are that you will not stay long in Rotterdam. It is a large and highly interesting workshop but it stresses the workshop characteristics to such an extent that the sight-seer, unless he be very fond of harbors and ships and dock-yards (a noble sight, I grant you, and highly interesting against the ever changing Dutch skies) will hardly spend more than a few hours in this village (in the New York sense of the word) built on the spot where the Rotte (a now defunct river) flowed into the Meuse (for the Rhine in Rotterdam is called the Meuse or Maas). You will probably decide to proceed to The Hague or Amsterdam. On your way to the station you will pass by the statue of Erasmus, the great laughing philosopher of the period immediately before the

Those who are "Cloister and the Hearth" fans will want
to visit Gouda with its charming and Gothic townhall.

outbreak of the Reformation, the best representative of that sound Dutch horse-sense which is such an excellent virtue unless one of the parents of the horse happens to be a donkey.

And so you are on your way to either The Hague or Amsterdam. I am no shareholder in the caravanserais of either city but as a strictly non-partisan outsider, I would advise you to spend first of all a few days in The Hague and then remove yourself and your chattels to Amsterdam. In that way you will see the life of the royal residence where everybody behaves as if he had nothing at all to do in this world except do nothing, and that of the legal capital of the Kingdom where the pace, according to Dutch standards, is both fast and furious.

Now, if you are new to Europe, let me give you another bit of advice. Make friends with the portier of your hotel, the man who looks like a vice-admiral in sky-blue. He is supposed to know everything, to hear everything, and to see everything (or the contrary, according to the needs of the moment) and almost invariably he does. Ask him for a small map of the town and then go to

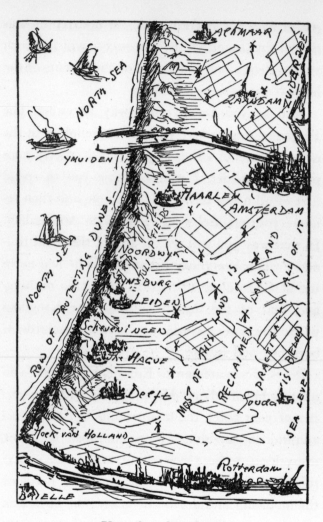

Your first four days.

the nearest café that looks inviting and sit you down and order yourself a cup of coffee or something else and study the lay of the land and the natives around you and make your plans.

If you still happen to be made of money (as all of us were a few years ago) you can of course hire cars to drive you to places. But if you are just a normal, every-day citizen, the street-cars will carry you to almost any given place of destination at a most reasonable remuneration. If you feel uncomfortable about traveling in a country where all the words look a mile long, ask the portier to write the number of the street-car line you may need on a piece of paper and also the name of the place you want to visit and show your slip of paper silently to the conductor who will then inform you in excellent English that he used to be a steward on a line between Newport News and Amsterdam and will ask you what you are obliged to pay for good Scotch nowadays. You will then answer that you think the Dutch a fine race, whereupon he will immediately respond with a fluent denunciation of everything Dutch and in that way you will spend an agreeable quarter of

Where to spend a morning in The Hague.

an hour until he tells you where to get off and please give his regards to his uncle William in San Francisco the next time you get back to your home in Cleveland.

Now, what should you see and what should you not see? Let me warn you beforehand that everybody in Holland, being constitutionally entitled to his or her own opinion which is quite as good and much better than mine, will tell you differently and will hint that I, as a dark ex-patriate, do not know what I am talking about. But if, when and how I have a couple of friends in Holland to whom I want to show the country at its best and in a minimum of time, then this is my own schedule.

I would leave my hotel at about ten o'clock. And I would first of all go to the Mauritshuis, the home of the last Dutch governor of Brazil and now one of the loveliest among the small museums of this or any other planet. It is exactly what a small museum should be. It only shows the very best and it shows it under the most favorable conditions. By the way, if you happen to be traveling with others, whenever you get to a museum do not

called it the Count's Lodge (Count is "Graaf" in Dutch and Lodge or Hedge was "haag" and there you have the riddle of that strange name, 's-Gravenhage.) The Ridderzaal in the center is the oldest part. It is now used for the meeting of the two houses of Parliament when they come together to listen to the Queen's annual message. To the right of the Ridderzaal, where today the Dutch Senate meets, is the spot (read your Motley!) where Johan van Oldenbarneveldt, the greatest statesman of the old Republic, was decapitated as a result of one of those ferocious and unpardonable theological disputes which disgrace almost every page of the history of the Old World.

All around you, two centuries ago, were the executive offices of those High and Mightinesses, the Estates General of the Republic of the United Seven Netherlands, who ruled the world of that day pretty much as they liked, and here you are in a spot which has been a seat of government for almost 700 consecutive years.

Now, if you have no further desire for museums (there are a raft of them and any local guide-book will tell you where to find them) I would advise you to take a street-car for Scheveningen. The street-car will follow the old road constructed by Huygens in the seventeenth century (the first road built through the dunes) and when you get to Scheveningen, have your lunch and do whatever you please, go swimming or take a nap or both.

After lunch take yourself a taxi and tell the chauffeur to show you the House in the Woods (now a Royal Palace) which is a lovely quiet spot where you will come face to face with the dignity of the seventeenth century as you will do in few other places, and then drive or walk through those woods, the only remnant of the mighty forest that in the days of the Romans ran all the way from Belgium to Denmark, and then walk back to town and once more sit ye down in some café and look at the life of this Dutch Washington, where the quiet streets remind you of New York on Yom Kippur.

If perchance you are interested in the most lucid mind the world has so far produced, then you might end your day by taking a taxi (for you

It was among villages like these that men like Spinoza
and Descartes spent their days and did their work.

won't find it so easily by yourself) and going to the house in which Spin za died, the house on the Paviljoensgracht 32. And when you reach that simple little room underneath the sloping roof where he polished his lenses and wrote his letters and his philosophies, give a thought to the glorious incongruities of this world. Here you stand in the presence of genius. And when fifty years ago they unveiled the statue just around the corner, they had to call out the reserves to protect the guests against the attacks of the enraged Calvinists.

I know that my method of traveling is not at all like the system practiced by the usual agencies of mass-transportation. But what earthly use in merely "seeing" a country? You must feel it, sense it, you must get hold of what sort of manner of men and women live in that particular spot, if you want your travels to be of lasting value to you. Personally when I travel I am all for taking it easy and doing a lot of sitting down. Coffee and mineral water are cheap and you need not drink them, but they allow you to sit and study the people, the policemen, the officers, the

This picturesque sort of bridge is rapidly disappearing.

girls, the endless bicyclists, the newspaper venders, the professors and the members of Parliament (brief-cases and whiskers), the panhandlers and some of your own compatriots wondering how they are going to kill time in a town where nothing ever seems to happen (to them nothing will ever happen anywhere). And in the evening the obliging portier will tell you whether there is a good concert, or if you cannot live without movies, you may see good new German or Russian pictures or the familiar American sort. Otherwise there are the cafés and the bars where the music is invariably good and sometimes excellent.

And then the next morning I would advise you to go to Haarlem. If you can afford a car, take one and tell the chauffeur to follow the coast as soon as he has left Leyden. Between The Hague and Leyden you will drive along a charming old road with lovely country houses (and with some very interesting new sorts of architecture). Just before you reach Leyden, when you get to the old mouth of the Rhine, tell the chauffeur to stop for a moment and then take a look at the distant city. For that was as far as the Spaniards ever got in their effort to take Leyden in 1574. Soon afterwards the Dutch cut the dykes of the Meuse and turned the whole southern part of the province of Holland into an inland sea. And they sailed their flat-bottomed scows between the deserted houses of hastily deserted villages and stormed the dykes behind which the Spanish troops were posted and dug still further gaps through still further dykes, until at last the salty waters of the North Sea were able to reach out toward that city where pestilence and courage and hunger and despair and obstinate tenacity were fighting a bitter fight for supremacy, until just in the nick of time the first of the relief boats carrying its cursing cargo of men, black with gunpowder and red with blood, came a-sailing across the tops of the willow trees, when those inside the town who could still stand or walk dragged themselves to the churches to thank Divine Providence for this miraculous token of grace, while the others grabbed at the food that was thrown to them from a thousand baskets and gorged on the first square meal they had had in four months.

Once inside the city you might stop a moment before the University, although there is not very much to be seen there. The stately canals of Leyden, however, are worth a visit for then you will suddenly begin to understand the life of a little university like this in which the actual university buildings are so few and simple and far between that any one of our most simple state universities would be ashamed if it had nothing better to show, and which nevertheless and notwithstanding has been the center of very serious learning for almost four centuries. Scholarship needs quiet. Well, quiet is the watchword of those canals.

And then on to Haarlem (returning to The Hague the same evening) through the tulip fields which are unfortunately never in bloom when most people visit Holland, and soon you will begin to see the outline of another city. It had been less fortunate than Leyden; for, during the War for Liberty, hunger had finally forced it to surrender and the men and women who had served in its defense were bound back to back and were drowned in the canals as a lesson to all

The Tower of Haarlem has become a landmark of the whole countryside.

other wicked rebels who dared to revolt against their Church and their anointed King.

The market-place in Haarlem is a pleasant place for luncheon, and when you have had your fried sole, go to the house which the charitably inclined burghers of the seventeenth century had built for their less fortunate neighbors when they were no longer able to provide for themselves. You need not greatly bother about the other pictures (although they are quite good) but I would advise you to go straight to the rooms in the rear of the building where Frans Hals hangs, and there you will meet some one who was probably the greatest virtuoso of the brush. What that incredible man did at the age of eighty (he died aged eighty-six but in his early eighties, after he had given up painting as an unlucrative profession for almost thirty years, he smeared these things together) is something so absurdly superior to almost anything done by any of his rivals that you will hardly know what to make of it.

And perhaps you will now begin to understand what I meant when I told you in my introduction that this is indeed a very strange land. It pro-

In Delft, little corners will remind you of Venice.

duces men like Hals and Rembrandt and does not know what to do with them. It lets them die in abject poverty. It appreciates the value of their work, and yet if they want to die in the poorhouse, that is their business.

Personally I know of no other place where I ever get quite such a shock of the suddenly revealed strength of pure beauty as right here, unless it be in that room in Florence where they keep the sculptures of Michelangelo. But such experiences as these are worth all the trouble of leaving home and mother and the old familiar scenes. They make life what it is or rather should be—a search for that ultimate revelation of beauty which borders upon the divine.

The next morning, if you still have time, you might visit Delft. The town will remind you of Vermeer, which is as it should be, for he lived here and painted here and died here in the usual way, insolvent. But in the old Prinsenhof, the ancient monastery which was given to William the Silent after he had lost all his personal fortunes in the struggle for independence, you will suddenly come face to face with historical reality.

Muiden—the literary castle.

For it was right here, on these stairs, that a hired assassin of Philip of Spain plugged two bullets through William's chest and it was right here that he died. In the near-by church there is his grave together with that of all the other members of that House of Orange which for almost four centuries has been such an integral part of the Low Countries that when the inevitable day comes when all kingdoms shall cease to be, the good people, voting for their first president, will probably have no other candidate than either the present Queen or one of her direct descendants.

The next morning you had better move on to Amsterdam. Your watch is your time-table. There is a train every half hour. They are electric trains, very comfortable and very clean and third class is perfectly all right. If it is tulip time, you will see the tulips even better from the high railroad dyke than from the flat road of the day before. And when you come near Amsterdam, watch the water of the canals. Water, water everywhere, and the water almost up to the top of the roads, which in most instances are also the dykes. On your right all the land, as far as your eye reaches,

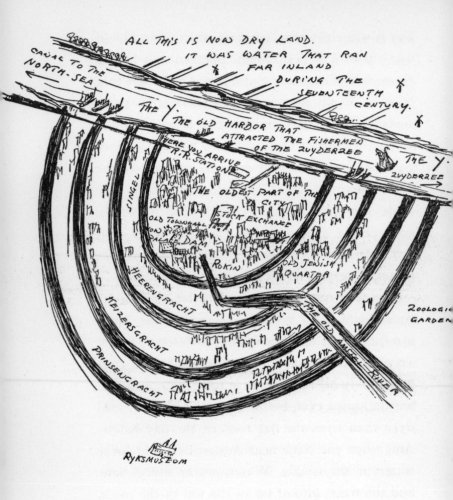

You can never lose your way in Amsterdam if you will
only remember that the city grew in a semi-circular
fashion with the Y as its base.

was until quite recently a part of the vast Haarlem Lake on which many important naval engagements were fought during the famous siege of Haarlem. And on your left the pastures are the bottom of the old Y which played such an important rôle in the history of Amsterdam, for it was not only the harbor of its ships but also an artery of trade which reached far inland and which was the industrial center of the Republic when all the work was done by wind-power.

The railroad station of Amsterdam was one of those unfortunate incidents which happen to most countries. It was built by people who were so delighted with their new inventions that they completely lost sight of the esthetic necessities of the day. The station completely cuts the city off from its water-front and as a result the town has turned its back upon itself and has moved southward and left the old business center and the railroad terminal high and dry somewhere in the north, as if to get even for the desecration of the stately beauty of the old harbor.

As a rule, whenever you get to a new city, it is a good thing to ask yourself first of all, "Exactly

how did this town get its start?" For once you
know how it began, you will have no further trouble with the topography. A single look at the map
will show you how Amsterdam originated. First
of all, in the twelfth century, a small fishing village on the old Y. That fishing village began to
spread inland with the boom in the herring indus-
try. Then came the period of prosperity and land
speculators bought up the available real estate to
build houses for the rapidly increasing population that came pouring into the Low Countries as
soon as they had gained their liberty, and pro-
claimed themselves (within reasonable bounds, of
course) a place of refuge for all those who in
their own countries suffered religious or economic
persecution.

Those new "out-lays," as they were called in
Dutch, ran in a semi-circle around the original
nucleus. They are today the stately canals known
as the Heerengracht and the Keizersgracht (the
Keizer, by the way, was the Emperor Charles V
who died in 1558 and not the present Kaiser Wil-
helm, as all-too-patriotic French passport officers
seemed to think when they treated the unfortu-

nate inhabitants of that most dignified street to an extra severe examination as suspicious neighbors of "le Kaiser"), and the Prinsengracht. It will amply repay you to take many walks along these Grachts. Indeed Amsterdam, like most watery cities, must be seen afoot in order to be really appreciated. Taxis go too fast. Besides at almost every moment you will be sure that your chauffeur is going to pitch you into a canal. Don't be scared, they never do, but it is just one of their little jokes, like that cracking of the neck, so dear to the hearts of otherwise harmless osteopaths. And so I would advise you to spend one whole day, just walking around. One of the things that will strike you is the general love for flowers. But people who live constantly beneath the sombre skies of these water-soaked regions have an extra need of such colorful companions.

There exists a myth about the love for color on the part of the Mediterranean nations. I am not so sure that they actually love color, they just happen to live in colorful countries, but, as a rule, they are quite as indifferent about their blessings as the hardy Swiss who placidly go on

You are now standing before the house of Rembrandt.

milking their cows and never give a look at their own mountain-peaks.

The higher up north you get, say Sweden or Lapland, the greater a love for flowers you will discover. And if the southern peoples really loved their flowers so dearly, it would hardly pay the Dutch to send their own cut-flowers to the Riviera by airplane, as they do and most profitably every day during the winter season.

As for the other local curiosities that may interest you, you had better consult your little guide book. I would suggest that sometime during the day you should spend perhaps half an hour in Rembrandt's ancient home, the one he had to leave when he was thrown into bankruptcy. It is pleasant to sit there in the little room and contemplate the sort of life that must have gone on in this house two and a half centuries ago. You may wonder how he could work in such dark rooms. But when he lived there, they were not dark. The house was then in a suburb, which was being rapidly populated by Jewish refugees from Spain and Portugal. Today the pants-factories all around it cut off most

The towers of Amsterdam are still the same as those
Rembrandt drew (only better).

of the light. But even so, a few quiet minutes in this house will tell you more about the man himself and his work than almost anything else I can think of. And look out of the windows into the street. The animated oriental life of that entire neighborhood has not changed very greatly since the days of Rembrandt. For Amsterdam is an essentially Jewish town because the quick and restless Jewish brain has strongly impressed itself upon the slower moving mentality of the original natives. As a result, Amsterdam has developed something which you will also find in New York, a queer and easy-come-easy-go sort of verbal give-and-take. There is more laughter here than in all other Dutch cities put together. An Amsterdam policeman or waiter or street-vender will see a joke a mile away. In the rest of the country they are only appreciated when they are a little hoary with age.

And then of course there is the Ryksmuseum, that vast storehouse of some of the greatest things that have ever been said with a brush. This museum, unless you handle it intelligently, may give you such an overdose of paint and canvas

When you see that well-known etching of Rembrandt's showing a view of Amsterdam it is interesting to remember that our own New Amsterdam grew directly out of that old one.

that it will spoil all your further interest in the arts. Therefore, if you can possibly do it, make a number of short trips to the Ryksmuseum. It costs you nothing and you should acquire the habit of walking in and out of museums as you would do in and out of your bank or an Italian church.

Incidentally, most people are rather fond of Zoos and the Amsterdam Zoo is well worth a visit. The aquarium for those who love aquariums (to me they are absolutely fascinating, but you never can tell) will be a veritable god-send on a rainy day when it is too dark to look at pictures.

And the odd gaps between going from one place to the next may be profitably filled in by making first-hand studies of the noble art of trick bicycle-riding. Those who are not absolutely perfect, get killed off very young. The survivors thereupon develop a perfection in the difficult technique of balancing which will fill your soul with deep envy. Sit you down on the Leidsche Plein or on the Rembrandt Plein and let the show pass by you while you are supposed to be writing postal cards to the dear family in

The landscape is flat but the sky is without limit.

Ithaca, N. Y. You won't write many, for you will be forever clutching your companion's hand and shouting, "Look at that girl carrying a potted palm on her shoulders!" or again, "Look at that family with five kids tucked away between the frame!" All very harmless and pleasant and the cost again is negligible.

Of course one whole day you will have to devote to the obligatory visit to Marken and Volendam. Now, so much has been written about the Coney Island aspects of the famous island in the Zuyder Zee and the equally famous village that people are apt to overlook the fact that if you care for flat landscapes beneath magnificent skies, the short voyage across the Zuyder Zee and through the canals will fill your mind with memories that will remain with you till the end of your days. Of course, you have got to have the breaks, from the angle of the weather. It must neither rain nor must the sun shine too brightly. But if you happen to choose an in-between day when the sun and the clouds are fighting cautiously for the mastery of the dome of Heaven, you will see something very much worth your

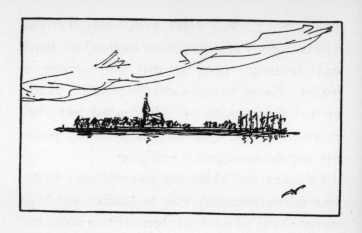

In the distance the Island of Marken hangs suspended
in mid-air.

while. And if you like that trip, you can arrange (ask the inevitable portier of the hotel) for a visit to the gigantic works that has turned the Zuyder Zee into an inland lake, and that will turn that inland lake eventually into dry land.

That expedition will account for another day and if you are not in a hurry (and why hurry? It does not matter how many countries you see, it matters how well you see a few of them), spend a further day taking a boat trip through the old industrial stronghold of Holland, the low regions of the Zaan, where two centuries ago windmills performed the endless tasks connected with the business of preparing the raw materials from the Indies into the finished product, ready for export. This trip, if I am not mistaken, will bring you to Alkmaar and if you choose the right day you will see more cheeses than you had ever dreamed could be eaten in a hundred years. And if you are a person of a very enterprising turn of mind, you might extend your voyage as far as the island of Texel, which is one of the loveliest islands of the North Sea and a paradise for those who make a hobby of birds. There are several

Once a week a small town like Alkmaar becomes a veritable beehive.

The tower of the town of Hoorn after which Cape Horn
has been called.

Don't expect to sleep in places like this every night. Such inns exist but they are off the beaten track.

good trains for Helder that will allow you to make the trip up and down in a single day. But if you want to spend more time on it, don't worry about your accommodations. The smaller country hotels are perfectly good and comfortable. They do not sell "The Saturday Evening Post" in the hall but Camels and Luckies are as cheap as in America. Only why smoke a foreign brand in a country that is almost made of tobacco and where you will soon discover a native brand that will suit your own individual taste?

For the rest, you will find them scrupulously clean and the meals, if you do not insist upon getting Philadelphia scrapple or Boston baked beans 4,000 miles away from home, will have only one fault. You won't be able to eat all they give you. After the third course you may decide to go out and come up for a little air. And here I want to give you a tip about something that few people seem to know about. The Official Information office for tourists in Holland will provide you with details.

Right across the Zuyder Zee lies a part of Holland that is but rarely visited. It is called Fries-

The old Dromedary Tower used to guard the harbor of
Enkhuizen.

land, because it was originally inhabited by
Frisians and not because it is so much nearer to
the North Pole than the rest of the Kingdom.
Friesland has very lovely lakes and it has good
sailing boats. If there are half a dozen of you
(or even fewer) you might make arrangements to
hire a sailing boat for a couple of days and start
upon an adventure which to most travelers is a
complete novelty.

There is no motion in this world comparable
to the smooth progress of a really good sailing
vessel. And for once you will be really the master
of your own destiny. You will sleep on board and
you will cook your own meals on board. And in
the evening you will stop near some quiet village
or on the banks of some peaceful lake and there
will be no elevated noises to disturb you and no
rumbling subways nor hooting sirens of fire-
engines to make the nights hideous. And you may
suddenly realize that a starry Heaven can be
more impressive than even the most colossal
scenic effect of the most colossal of our movies.
And furthermore you will be initiated into an
entirely new world of actions and reactions. You

The Tower of the Dome of Utrecht is only one-third as
high as the Empire State Building but it is visible far
and wide in this flat land.

will learn to think quickly and you will get familiar with new risks that never entered into your former realm of possibilities. Not very dangerous risks. But bumping into bridge-heads or ducking before the obstinate sail that has tried to push you overboard are pleasant and novel experiences to those whose lives thus far have been regulated entirely by the change from red lights to green ones.

Those who are averse to roughing it and who prefer a more genteel mode of travel and who want to see something new that has not become completely hackneyed and postal-cardy, should see the Official Tourist office about a trip through another part of Holland that is but rarely seen by foreign eyes. The eastern provinces are entirely different from their western neighbors. As I told you, when you take the train from Amsterdam or The Hague to Germany, you will be among the flat meadows until you reach Utrecht, the oldest town of Holland, situated in the heart of the country from where its mighty tower overlooks half the Kingdom. But the moment you pull out of the Utrecht station, the landscape changes completely and you are among the sandy hills of the great European plain that, following the shores of the Baltic, runs all the way from here to the Ural Mountains which separate Russia from Siberia. But the Dutch, who are specialists in detail, have turned these eastern provinces into one large park which is entirely in keeping with their national feeling for things that shall be done soberly, unostentatiously and apparently for all the ages to come.

I know that there are a lot of people to whom I never would give this advice, for these characteristics are so utterly foreign to our own tastes that such citizens will speedily die of boredom when doomed to spend a couple of nights in Arnhem or Nymegen or Deventer. But that is because they approach them from the wrong angle. After all, every country should be judged by what the inhabitants get out of it. The visitor from abroad merely comes to spend a few hours or days, then the dogs bark and the visitor from abroad passes on, never to return.

But how does that life, too slow and even-flowing for a hustling go-getter, suit the people

who have no desire for anything else? Well, it
suits them just about perfectly. They would be
miserably unhappy in one of our up-and-coming
cities of the Middle West, but they like this sort
of existence. Now please remember that I am
not saying that one form of life happens to be
right when all others are wrong. They are both
of them but manifestations of the same human
spirit which tries to achieve some sort of content-
ment during its short stay upon this planet. And
those who have eyes and ears for interesting and
subtle varieties of happiness will derive a great
deal of pleasure from just such an unobtrusive
voyage of discovery as I here suggest. As for the
others, they have long since asked themselves,
"Ah, what is he talking about anyway?" and
they are by now ordering their seventh *fine* in
the Dôme or the Rotonde of Paris. I wish them
luck. I have nothing against either the Dôme or
the Rotonde, but that is a different story again.

Now if you will look for a moment at the map
(and count that day of the faithful pilgrim lost
when he does not spend at least a quarter of an
hour window-traveling by means of a good map)

At small expense you can start on a voyage of discovery
which few people have made.

you will see that in the southern part of Holland there are still two other provinces which are known as Brabant and Limburg. They are the step-children of the old Dutch Republic. During the great rebellion of the sixteenth century the people of Brabant and Limburg remained faithful to the mother church and therefore continued to recognize the rule of the Spaniards. When much against everybody's expectations the northern rebels were victorious, these two provinces remained in Dutch hands as a sort of "conquered territory" which had few rights and a great many duties. The inhabitants spoke the same language as the conquerors but they cordially detested their new Calvinistic masters and as a result they developed many of the characteristics of the Irish after their island had become an English dependency. They did not share in the era of prosperity of the North. Their cities maintained an almost mediaeval aloofness from the rest of the busy world, but the people who lived in Bois-le-Duc (it is 's Hertogenbosch in Dutch, but the English maps usually give the French name) and Maastricht retained a much more human attitude

In Drente mysterious piles of heavy stones—the graves
of prehistoric heroes—show that this part of the country
must have been inhabited several thousand years ago.

towards life than the good Calvinists of the North who never could drop that schoolmasterly, holier-than-thou attitude which (as I told you before) is at once their strength and their weakness, for while it makes them tenacious of purpose, it also gives them a rigidity of outlook which does not make for an easy or pleasant social life.

As a matter of fact, to the average American who travels to gather new impressions and who is an addict of the good old American philosophy that life is too short to bother unduly about all our neighbors' mis-doings, the atmosphere of Bois-le-Duc and especially of Maastricht will come as a pleasant relief from the rather forbidding perfection of the North. He will discover much in these parts that takes him back to the Middle Ages and even to the days of the Romans, who settled down in these parts while the North was still an almost uninhabitable marshland. He will be surprised by the gap that exists when it comes to the sixteenth, seventeenth and eighteenth centuries. But the trip, which will only take him three or four days (the roads are excel-

The city of Dordrecht is so old that you ought to see it
at night just after the sun has gone down.

lent for motoring) will be instructive as well as pleasant. At small cost and no inconvenience at all he will for once come face to face with the terrible racial and religious problem which the twentieth century has inherited from the previous nineteen hundred years.

Today the people of Brabant and Limburg are a loyal part of the Kingdom of the Netherlands. But step-children (step-children in the unfortunate sense of that most unfortunate word) never quite get over their experience. These step-children, however, are of a happy natural disposition. They are accustomed to a simple mode of living. They are industrious (it is a land of vast factories). They have a sense of humor. The rest you will have to find out for yourselves.

But if you feel that you cannot afford either the time or the money for this side-trip to the east and prefer to see what is usually called "something typically Dutch," then after you leave Amsterdam I would suggest that you take a train one afternoon for Dordrecht and spend the rest of the afternoon and the night there. Ask the portier to find out for you on what days the

The tall tower of Middelburg known as "Long John"
dominates the entire Island of Walcheren.

boat from Rotterdam to Middelburg passes through Dordrecht. And arrange your trip in such a way that the next morning you can take that boat from Dordrecht. It will take you most of the day until about six in the afternoon, but you will see such waterscapes as you can see in no other part of the world and you will get familiar with a vast variety of vessels and birds and bridges and fishermen and finely tinted distant dykes that will stand out as one of the high spots of your entire visit.

Most people nowadays arrange their visit to Zeeland (that is the province of which Middelburg is the capital, the mother-country of the New Zealand at the other end of the world) in such a way that they get there on Thursday when it is market-day. Unfortunately that market-day has become a sort of joy-ride for all the dear summer-guests of the Belgian seaboard and as a result the respectable farmers of these islands now shun their own market-day just because they happen to be respectable farmers and see no reason why they should be expected to parade as

111

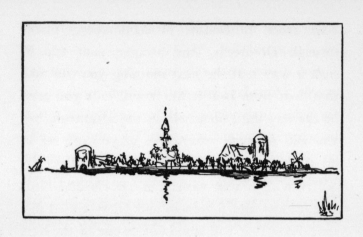

Veere.

a free show for complete strangers right on their own ancestral soil.

But if you reach this island on any other day except Thursday, you will be more than repaid for your little detour. If you can still ride a bicycle, you might well hire one and set forth on a trip across the island of Walcheren on which Middelburg is situated. The inevitable Dutch Bicycle Society will once more take you in hand and will tell you exactly where you are going and how long it will take you to get there. You can do the whole island in one day, but two would be better, especially if you are out of training.

There are the old cities like Flushing and Domburg and Veere and a vast number of small villages which will make you wonder whether the feudal order of living did not enjoy certain pleasant advantages over the order of living of today. There is undoubtedly a local tourist agency that will give you the details for such a trip. And if you should happen to enjoy playing Stanley, you might penetrate into the hinterland and get yourself ferried across to the other islands and visit Zierikzee or Goes and make those cities the center of your further peregrinations. You will find the people to be cordial and well-disposed towards strangers (except on Thursday, but then there is a reason). And you will see places which I do not believe have been visited by a dozen Americans since Thomas Jefferson learned to play the fiddle.

And from Zeeland, if you want to see the civilization of the Low Countries before the northern part took the lead, you can, by crossing the Scheldt, and by taking a bus or a tram, easily reach both Bruges and Ghent, the two Flemish towns that during the fifteenth century were as important as the Republic of the United Netherlands happened to be in the seventeenth.

Or you can take one of the trains that connect with the daily boats that ply between Flushing and England and go directly to Germany or Austria. Or you can sail within a few hours from Flushing to London on probably the most comfortable aquatic connections that run between England and the Continent. Or you can take an early morning train and be in Brussels or Paris only a few hours later. So that you need not feel that you have separated yourself from the rest of the world and will never see your loved ones again. On the contrary, that is one of the beauties of this small triangle of land, that you can get almost anywhere else in less than no time.

And what is the moral of the story? Well, there is not any. Those who continue to regard Europe as a picturesque peep-show for modern, progressive Americans who travel eastward to impress upon the natives of that effete continent the superior advantages of their own virile attitude towards life will merely have wasted their time. But they would have wasted their time no matter where they had gone, for Europe is not impressed by what they want to tell it. Europe does not even bother to listen, or shrugs its shoulders and answers, "Yeah, we have heard all that before, in the twelfth century or in the ninth, and it did not work then either."

Those who believe that a trip abroad should be an endless series of captain's dinners with funny paper caps and imitation jazz and odes to the perfection of the American Girl, will also make for the nearest exit and will try and find the real article (the phonier this real article in Europe happens to be, the more "real" it seems to them) in the Rue Pigalle or in Biarritz or some other place frequented by the late aristocracy of Spain and Montevideo.

But I was not talking to either of those groups. I was thinking of that rapidly increasing number of my fellow citizens who have learned some sort of lesson during the last four years, a lesson that makes them ask very seriously whether we ourselves were entirely on the right track when we went in for size and speed and hurry and who, exhausted by a pace that was much too fast for most of them, are now seriously endeavoring to find some way out that should provide us with a "mode of living" rather than a chance to "make a living."

They may find it here. They may find it here all the more because this part of the world, two hundred years ago, was exactly what we ourselves were only a very short time ago, the center of a new world, the leader in all branches of commerce and science and the arts. In science and commerce we have done more than our share. In the arts, not quite so well. But all that belongs to the realm of speculative philosophy and I am supposed to be writing a guide-booklet.

Just now what we need so terribly badly is a new point of view about ourselves and a new angle of vision about our own future. We will soon be obliged to take a little stock for the future and we will have to order and regulate our ideas very carefully if we want to lay firm foundations for a better and happier future.

If you are a mere sight-seer, this booklet will do you very little good. But if you are somewhat of a "seer" in a slightly different sense of the word, these few pages may not have been a sheer waste of time. At least, I hope so.